What would you like to CHANGE?

Published by Wisdom of the Whole Coaching Academy LLC
1333 Webster Street Ste. A106
Alameda, CA 94501
1-510-864-2006
www.wisdomofthewhole.com

About the Wisdom of the Whole Coaching Academy:
The Wisdom of the Whole Coaching Academy is an international organization on the leading edge of holistic coaching, bringing the Wisdom of the Whole® model to transform and expand the coaching and learning paradigm. We are a home for discovery and exploration of a new way of coaching that creates wholeness and benefits the coach, the client, and the world. We are a school with heart and integrity, led by our visionary leader, Linda Bark, PhD, RN, MCC, NC-BC, NBC-HWC, a pioneer in the field of professional coaching.

ISBN-13: 978-0692982495
ISBN-10: 0692982493

First printing: November 7, 2017

What would you like to CHANGE?

Linda Bark

Robert Boisson

WISDOM OF THE WHOLE
COACHING ACADEMY

Contents

We dedicate this book to all
who aspire to know themselves
better, building awareness and
changing for the good of all.

How to Use This Book

Most books are just to be read; some are quick-glance guides; others are just to color.

But not this one.

This book cries out for you to look through it, read again, think and ponder, color or draw, add notes, quotes, and more. By adding your own changes, you will have begun the change process — a process that can then be applied outside the book.

Change begins here:

1.   Find a picture and matching words that grab your attention or pique your curiosity about something you would like to explore and/or change.

2.   We suggest that you delve into the words and artwork for possibilities. Become involved with them. Look for ways they might relate to you personally, or how they "speak" to you. Have fun and explore new ways to personalize the pages…modify, enhance, add, create. Make copies of pages and practice on them first if you want. This is your own unique, personal book.

Here are possibilities to consider in your exploration and to ignite your creativity:

More About a New Way to Change

"The significant problems we face cannot be solved at the same level of thinking we were at when we created them." —Albert Einstein

This book identifies a new process for dealing with challenges, problems, and change. You can change easier and faster if you come from different ways of knowing.

When people can explore their feelings, thoughts, images, body sensations, and sense of purpose, they move faster and make decisions that are aligned with their whole selves and everything around them. When they use this process, they don't lose momentum or motivation over time. In fact, just the opposite happens: they are engaged and excited about their progress and take one step after another until they reach their goals.

You will find four sections in this book — Source, Intuitive, Mythical, and Mental dimensions. These sections provide you the opportunity to look at parts of your life from different perspectives. We invite you to use different perspectives, or ways of knowing, to help you open doors for change. When you are ready, find out how the four dimensions of your world fit together by looking at pages 95 to 101.

This approach is based on a model developed by Jean Gebser (1905-1973), a German philosopher and poet, who is best known for a masterful work detailing historical change in human consciousness as people evolved (see Gebser's book *The Ever-Present Origin,* 1985 English translation). He pointed out four structures of awareness or consciousness with each leading to a new way of knowing. The sum of these different perspectives comes together and forms a new way of knowing called the Integral (wholeness) structure of consciousness.

Let us know what changes for you

Share your insights, ideas, and pictures with us at: *change.wisdomofthewhole.com.*

To join our sharing community, simply enter the book code: CHANGE7777

See what others uncovered or brought to light.

This is your book.

Read, think, then transform the drawings any way that you want. The possibilities are endless. The four drawings on the next page are examples of how the "Love yourself" illustration on page 15 might be changed and personalized.

"As I began to love myself, I freed myself of anything that is no good for my health— food, people, things, situations, and everything that drew me down."

"As I began to love myself I recognized that my mind can disturb me and make me sick. But as I connect it to my heart, my mind became a valuable ally. Today, I call this connection Wisdom of the Heart."

— Charlie Chaplin

(from a poem attributed to charlie chaplin having writing it on his 70th Birthday)

11

Source Dimension

This area of our lives is about knowing and being connected to something larger than ourselves such as nature, a divine being, creative energy, a religion, Source, love, all things, or everything.

Love yourself

What would be different in your life if you loved yourself more? If you don't love yourself, who will? If you don't love yourself, how will you let others' love in? How could you connect more to love? Love is at the center of connection to Source.

One way to explore these questions is to play with this page and the drawing. You don't need to be an artist. You are invited to write, color, and add in any way you like.

Source

You are invited to write, color, and add in any way you like.

15

Human beings, not human doings

We often ignore or resist the "being" side of ourselves that connects with Source, and instead, we focus on the "doing" part (and there is nothing wrong with doing). Do you want change in this area? If so, how could you change, even in a small way? How would your life be different if you had more balance between being and doing?

Use these pages to explore your balance between being and doing.

How are you impacted by discrimination?

Discrimination is about separation. It is the opposite of oneness and of connection to something larger than yourself where everything is unified, equal, and included.

What words, images, colors, patterns, insights, feelings, and body sensations come to you as you consider this question, connection to Source, and the accompanying drawing?

Feel free to express yourself on these two pages.

How do you resolve conflicting right values?

What are conflicting right values? You may have one important value and another that opposes the first. What is one example in your life? How can you resolve this? How could the conflicting right values be friends and work together?

Source

See what comes out as you add to these pages.

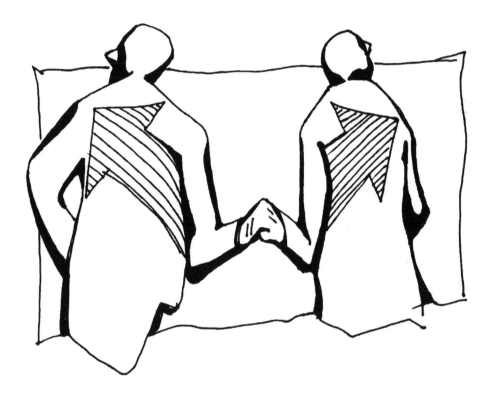

Compassionate,
not judgmental

Connection to Source can produce compassion. When in compassion, judgment is blocked. Is it true that the more compassionate you are with yourself, then the more compassionate you will be with others? People can sense when you come from judgment and that limits their openness, exploration, acceptance, and autonomy.

How would you feel about this drawing if the cat had some feathers sticking to its mouth?

What do you want to do on these pages?

Gratitude:
it feels so good

Do you want to be happier, more calm, and satisfied with your life? Finding ways to be grateful is an easy way to link to Source and achieve these goals. When people are grateful, they can be more motivated, see things from a fresh perspective, and experience more excitement about living.

You are invited to write down five things you are grateful for each day, and/or keep a gratitude journal every day for a month.

You can tell us the results of your journaling or post any of your pages on our book's website: *change.wisdomofthewhole.com*

Source

Play with these pages.

Do unto others as THEY would like to be done unto

Some call this the Platinum Rule and feel that it is an even better way to support others than using the Golden Rule of "Do unto others as you would like to be done unto." It shifts perspective from "I know what you want or need" to "What do you want or need?" Try it. What shifts within the relationship? What is the outcome? How is this result connected to Source?

How can experimenting with these pages start a shift you want to make?

Silence:
connection, rest,
meditation, prayer

Silence allows for deeper living. Insights come out of silence to enrich, inform, and change perspectives. How comfortable are you with silence? What would happen if you spent 10 percent more time in silence?

What do you want to do with these pages?

Cleansing is sacred

Letting go and lightening up can more easily enable your connection with Source. What no longer serves you? How can you let it go? What will be left? What will be enhanced?

Maybe you don't know why you want to draw a line here or a line there, write a word, use a certain color, or add a particular picture to the page. You are invited to let it come out, and let go. If you'd like, trace or make a copy of your favorite pages to experiment with first.

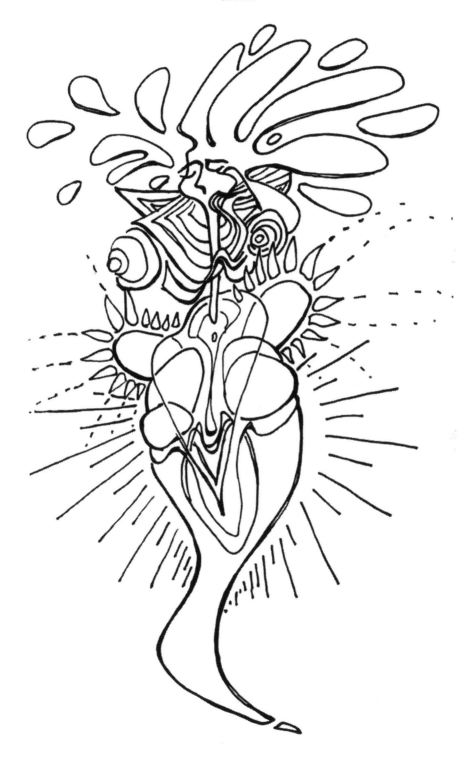

How are you violent to yourself?

This is an important question. Sit with it. Ask yourself about it. Be honest. Look inside. Ask others how they see you being violent to yourself. How can you stop it? How will your life change? We really don't have to hurt ourselves and suffer. You can if you want, but suffering doesn't seem to fit with Source and love.

If you hear your critical voice, be assured you can't "mess anything up" on these pages!

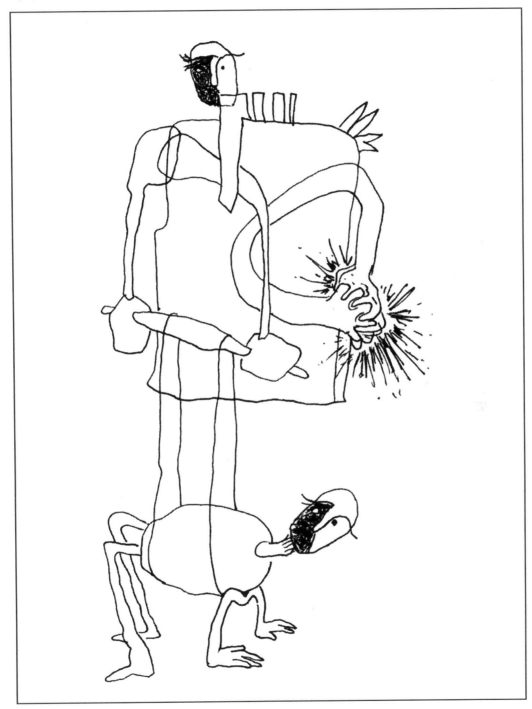

Synchronicity: when you know things are right

Sometimes things come together fast. You might feel in the "flow" of things. It is easy. There's no resistance. It feels like the right actions are happening. How could you be in the "flow" more often? What sense do you make of synchronicity? Does it connect you with Source or vice versa? What would your life be like if you were in the "flow" twice as much?

Amazing things can happen when you doodle in a "free form" way.

Self-Care Fun

How can taking care of yourself be fun? How can you shift from having it be a burden to a place of joy? This can be part of your self-love.

How could you have fun with these pages?

Walking the talk

Your inner mirror lets you see how your actions match your values and what is important to you. How do you feel when you become disconnected from your values? What do you want to change to feel more aligned with your talk?

How could you color, draw, write, or doodle about your alignment?

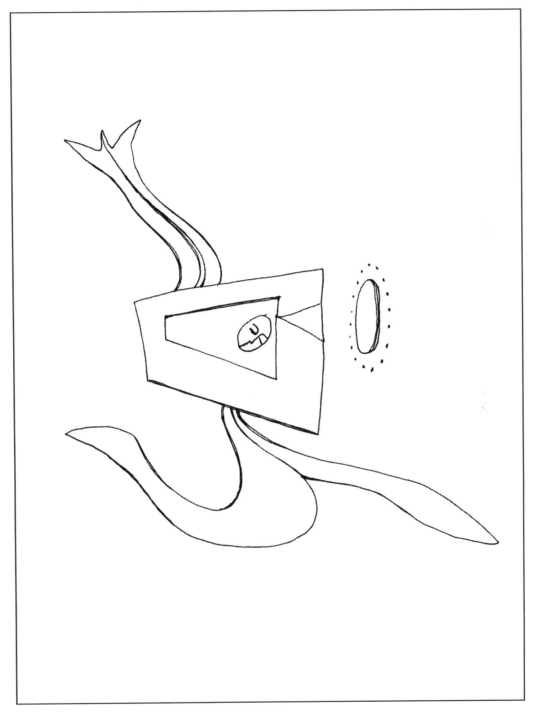

There's no time, no space in Source

This is the place of "all is well." Once you are able to arrive within this peaceful place, you might find it difficult to leave.

Source

How can you represent this space on these pages?

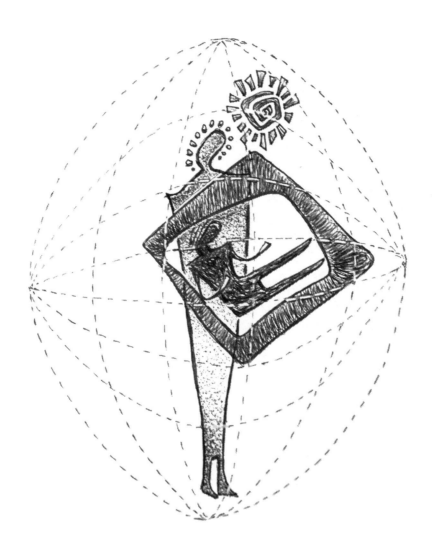

Intuitive Dimension

This area of our lives is based on subtle
information or ways of knowing.

Creativity:
it is you

Feel it. Love it. Be it. Rejoice in It. Share it.
It often comes from a fun, intuitive place.

How could you be creative on these pages?

Fun and games

How could you have more fun? More pleasure? More lightness? More humor? More ease? How much can you allow? How could you have 20 percent more? What stops you? What encourages you? Who is your tribe? What playmates do you want to invite? Tribe and community are essential parts of the Intuitive dimension.

How could you have fun with these pages?

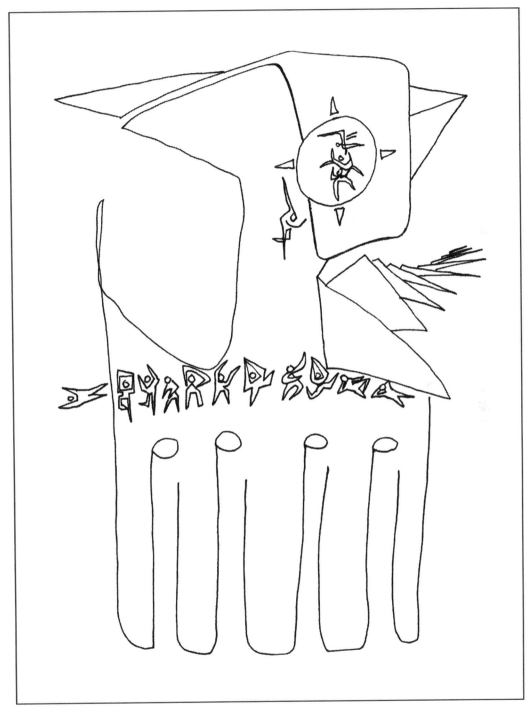

What if you believed in magic?

When you were three or four years old, you believed in magic. What about now? What if you really believed in magic? Who and what would be in your life, and who and what would be out of your life? This is a game changer, a consciousness changer, a life changer.

How about making some magic on these pages?

What is magic?

Go deep inside to answer this question. How do you use your intuition to make magic?

Intuitive

Write, color, doodle, draw magic.

Have you used your magic wand today?

Use it and see outside of the box. See new possibilities. Have more fun. Limits disappear. Try it. What happens? What doesn't happen? This could be one way to easily tap into your intuition.

Share what happens when you use your magic wand.

Sex magic

It's easy to feel magic and a different state of consciousness when in sex energy. What could change for you in this space?

Add to these pages.

Time is a single point in the Intuitive

In this space of intuition, energy, and magic, time is one-pointed, or unified, so that everything can happen at the same time. For example, this allows for ritual to affect past, present, and future.

How could you share your experience of this time frame in these pages?

Mythical Dimension

This area of our lives involves a way of being and knowing that is based on myths, roles, archetypes, storytelling, dialog, and different parts of ourselves.

What is your
life story?

Write about your past, what is happening now, and what you want to happen in the future. It is best to write in the third person as it gives you an outsider's perspective into your life. Use a magic wand and see what can change in your life story. Re-write or re-draw or re-dance your story from different perspectives. How would it be if you saw yourself as hero, criminal, victim, royalty, pioneer, warrior, or some other archetype?

Share the different perspectives of your story on these pages.

What is the story about your body?

Do you like the story? How do you want to transform your story? Changing your story can be a tool to change your body.

Want to play with these pages? You don't need to be an artist. You can use stick figures to illustrate changes.

Tell your story.

Blind spots

How can you find your blind spots? Everyone has them, and they work underground, unchecked. Blinds spots can form a base or pattern for our stories, perceptions, and actions. Being aware of your blind spots can give you an advantage.

How can you add your blind spots to these pages?

Who is your superhero?

What does your choice of superhero say about you? Your superhero or archetype can represent parts of you or qualities that you might want to embrace and embody. How does becoming more like your superhero or archetype change you?

How could you add your superhero to these pages?

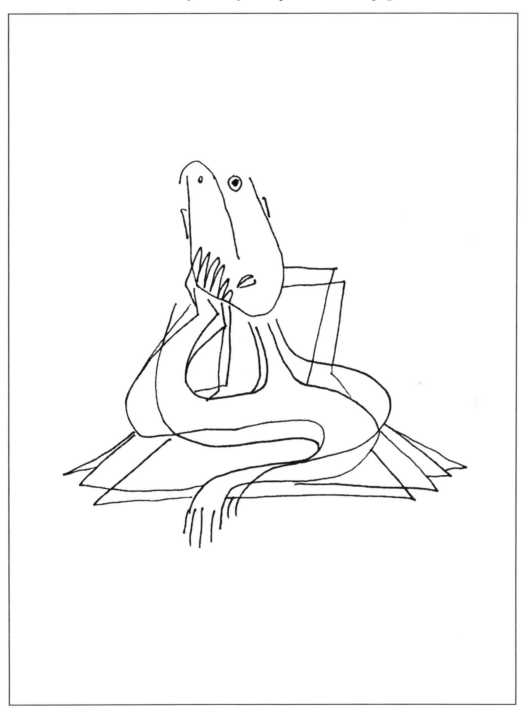

What is the most frequent role you play?

Are you helper, victim, hero, leader, bully, teacher, student, parent? What is your least frequent role? What part of you is in the shadows, least lived, or exposed? Where does it live in your being? How does hiding it hinder you? How could you accept it and not necessarily act it out?

There is no right or wrong way to add to these pages.

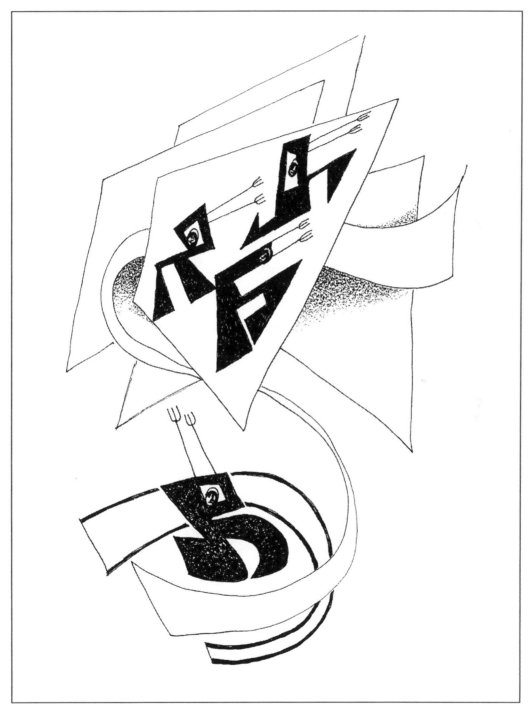

What "you" is emerging?

Are you resisting it? Are you welcoming it? Is it inevitable? What will help it emerge? Previous pages in this section might have prompted new ideas, thoughts, feelings, body wisdom, or sense of purpose.

How can these pages help the "new you" become clearer?

Time is a rhythm or season in the Mythical

In the Mythical Dimension, time is experienced in cycles and repeating patterns. Sunrise and sunset, seasons, moon phases, the tides, birth, life, and death are all examples. If you are relating to time in this way, you are in the Mythical. How can you use this sense of time to change your life? Have you experienced miscommunication when people used different definitions of time?

Try adding examples of your favorite cycles to these pages.

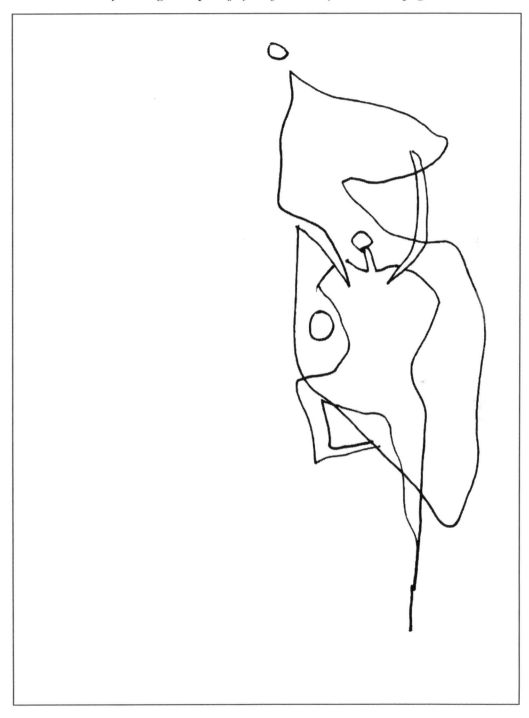

Mental Dimension

This area of our lives is a place of being and knowing which is based on logical, sequential, critical, and mechanistic thinking.

Old pattern,
new pattern

When deciding to change a current behavior, labeling it as an "old pattern" moves it into play. It is not who you are. It is not part of your personality. You might not need to go back to how it started or who else was involved in the creation, such as mother, father, minister, or sibling. You could start from now and go into the future. What is the old pattern? What is the new pattern? Learning how to go from the "old behavior" to the "new behavior" can be part of the exploration and planning. Sequential thinking is part of this dimension. What old patterns do you want to change?

Feel free to write and draw on these pages.

Resistance

In this dimension, movement progresses sequentially A to B to C to D. What flavor of resistance do you use to stop moving forward? Do you get busy, obsess, escape, justify, deny, or blame? How can you identify when you want to limit your time in resistance and when resistance can be your friend?

Are you resistant to make these pages your own?

Ambivalence:
a decision to not
make a decision

Ambivalence stops forward movement.
Do you feel pulled in opposing ways?
What do you do to resolve ambivalence?

When deciding how to personalize these pages, which way wins out?

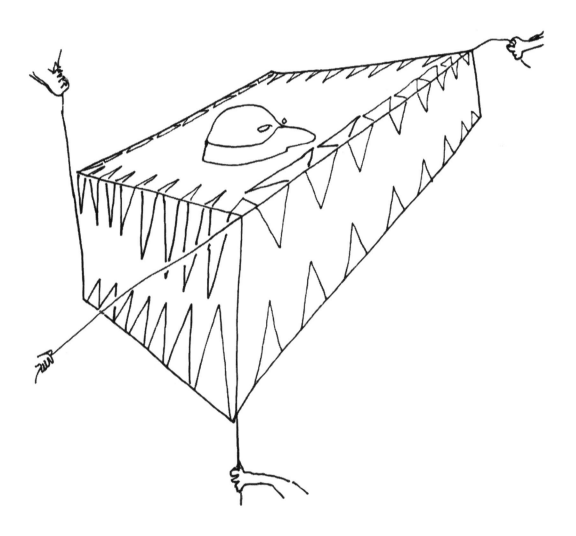

Autonomy can empower

"I can do it!" "I can move forward!"

Choose what you want for these pages.

Fear:
what scares you?

There are many theories about fear—what it is, how to address it, and how to get rid of it. Some rationalize fear and reason it out. What do you do when you are afraid? What would you like to do instead? Where does fear live in your body? How can fear be an ally?

Don't be afraid to add to these pages.

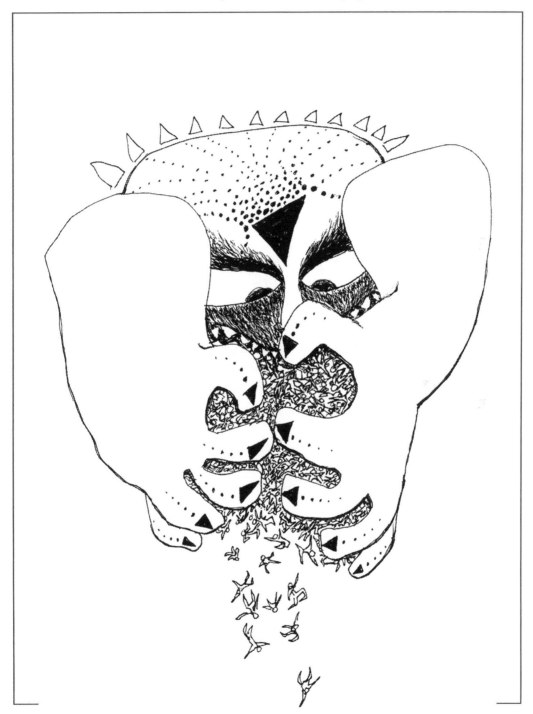

Money

Money, as we know it today, is a construct in the Mental dimension for measuring value. What is your relationship with money? Do you feel as though you have enough? What is enough? How do you receive it? What do you want to do with it?

Mental

How much would you charge for your additions to these pages?

What question, if asked, would change your life for the better?

How can you find this question? Once you've found it, what is an easy, next step towards this change? Asking these kind of questions can come from a logical, analytical, mental perspective.

Write, draw, doodle, and/or color your answer.

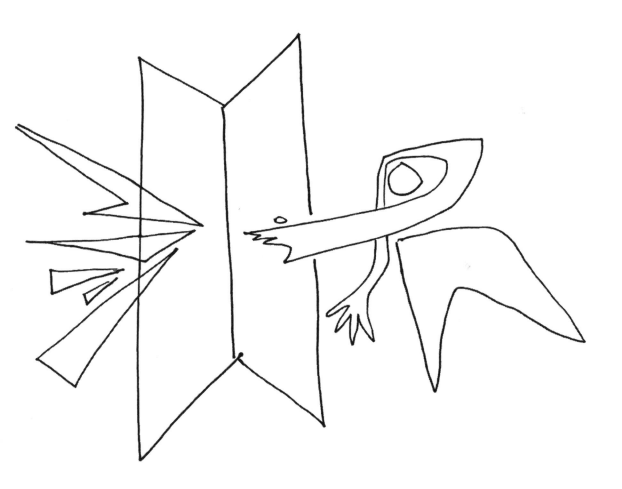

The journey of 10,000 miles begins from where you are standing (not from the first step) –Yi Wu

What values do you stand on? What philosophy informs your way of being? These are far-reaching, deep concepts. Is there anything you would like to change?

Where are you standing on your journey?

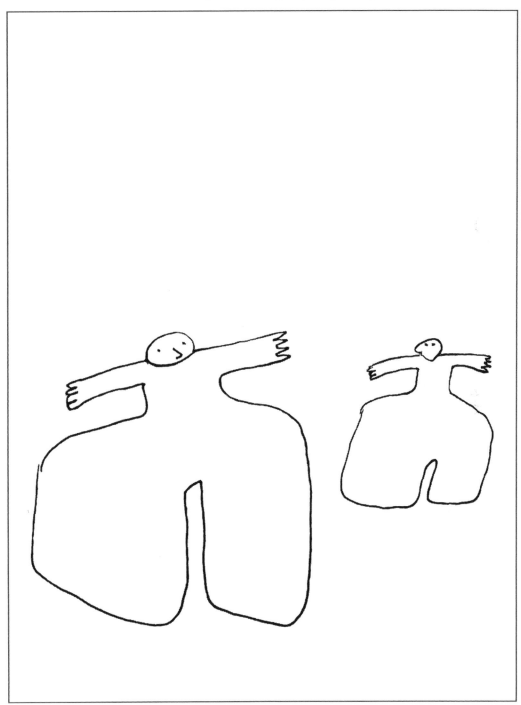

Time is lineal in the Mental:
past, present, & future

Even though it's difficult to think about anything but lineal time, time is different in other dimensions and helps you know what dimension you are in. How do you live within and move outside of lineal time?

What is your experience of time when adding to these pages?

Pulling All the Dimensions Together: Wisdom of the Whole®

When your inner knowing comes from several dimensions, you are more accepting of other people's perspectives (your external worlds). As you turn outward, you can appreciate multiple, non-violent perspectives on any topic, celebrate differences, acknowledge individual gifts and skills, and discover how individuals complement one another in a group, whether it is a family, healthcare team, or division of a company.

An integral approach, using all the dimensions of inner knowing, not only brings comfort with and appreciation of differences, but also awareness of similarity, connection and being part of a whole. People are less likely to harm each other because they realize the extent of their connection and oneness. Metaphorically speaking, they are not inclined to use the left hand to cut off the right hand. This could result in less violence and could create more kindness, caring, and consideration for one another and the planet we live on.

How are these dimensions alive in you?

Sketch/write your thoughts in the boxes below.

Source:

Being and knowing, in which you are connected to something larger than yourself such as nature, a divine being, creative energy, a religion, Source, love, all things or everything

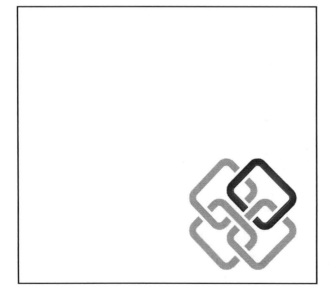

Intuitive:

A way of being which is based on subtle information or ways of knowing

The four dimensions intertwine and amplify each other; the whole is greater than the sum of the parts. One structure is not seen as more important; rather, they're all important, and accessing the gifts from each of them allows for a more fulfilling experience. Time, space, and causality are not constrained.

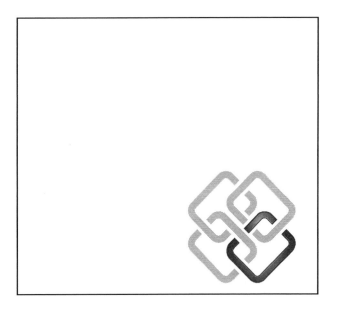

Mythical:

A perspective of being and knowing which is based on myths, roles, archetypes, storytelling, dialog, and different parts of ourselves

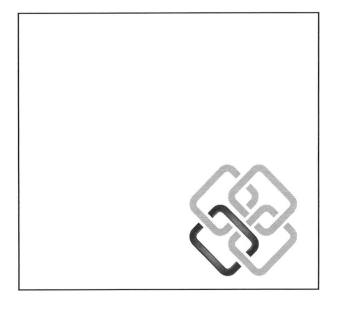

Mental:

A place of being and knowing which is based on logical, sequential, critical, and mechanistic thinking

Source + Intuitive + Mythical + Mental = The Wisdom of the Whole

Using all the dimensions can help you and others move more quickly and authentically toward goals. Using approaches from various quadrants accesses different parts of the self. Drawing from all four quadrants allows the whole person to be addressed and connections between the different parts of oneself to become clear. What connections do you see?

Wisdom of the Whole® Movement Exercise

Here is a different way to understand and connect the four dimensions of your world that combine to create the Wisdom of the Whole®. This approach is based on a model developed by Jean Gebser (1905-1973), a German philosopher and poet, who is best known for a masterful work about the evolution of human consciousness over millions of years (see Gebser's book *The Ever-Present Origin,* 1985 English translation). He pointed out four structures of awareness or consciousness with each leading to a new way of knowing. The sum of these different perspectives comes together and forms a new way of knowing called the Integral (wholeness) structure of consciousness.

We invite you to "try on" these different dimensions or parts of your life. This exercise incorporates imagination and physical movement to help you experience the dimensions at a systematic, unified, and deeper level.

To begin, find a quiet place, take a breath, and shift into a space of less words and more images, sensations, and feelings. This exercise will take about 10-20 minutes depending how long you want to stay in each of the dimensions.

1. Take this book and go to a corner of the room that you are in. Consider this to be the corner for experiencing Source. This is the place where all is well, where you are connected to all that you need. Take a deep breath. Stay in this corner for several minutes. What do you sense in your body as you inhabit this corner? What images come to mind? Close your eyes and feel this experience.

2. When you are ready to "try on" another dimension, move clockwise to the second corner of the room and pretend that millions of years pass by as you step to the next corner. This will be the Intuitive/Energy/Magic corner. Experience this new place. Here, tribe is fundamental, and people use subtle ways of knowing rather than language to communicate. In this place, intuition and sensitivity to energy are useful, and there is still a close connection to nature and Source. Ritual is richly used, and there is no sense of time or space. Take a deep breath. Stay in this corner for several minutes. What do you sense in your body in this corner? What images come to mind? Close your eyes, and feel the Intuitive/Energy/Magic dimension.

3. When you are ready to "try on" another dimension, move clockwise to the third corner of the room and pretend that millions of years pass by as you step to the next corner. This will be the Mythical corner. Experience this new

dimension that now, for the first time, incorporates space and time. Here, space is known as what is above, below, and within which all things exist and move. Time is attuned to the sun and the seasons. There is more language. Story and myths describe what is happening. Take a deep breath. Stay in this corner for several minutes. What do you sense in your body as you inhabit this corner? What images come to mind? Close your eyes, and feel the Mythical dimension.

4. When you are ready to "try on" another dimension, move clockwise to the last corner of the room and pretend that hundreds of years pass by as you step to the next corner. This will be the Mental corner. Experience this new place, realizing that this is the place where logical, sequential thinking lives. Here, small parts are seen more often than the whole. This is where things are often considered to be material, devoid of energy. Duality is rampant (i.e. yes or no, good or bad, etc.), and time is lineal. This is where measurements are taken, and where plans and lists are made. Take a deep breath. Stay in this corner for several minutes. What do you sense in your body as you inhabit this corner? What images come to mind? Close your eyes, and feel the Mental dimension.

5. When you are ready, move to the center of the room. Consider this the Wisdom of the Whole® area, and imagine that you can hold and easily access all the other corners from the middle of the room. How does this feel? What do you sense in your body as you inhabit this space? What changes as you live in this space? Take a deep breath. Stay in the center of the room for several minutes. Close your eyes, and feel how joining the dimensions allows for rich knowing and being.

6. Below are some questions to consider after the exercise. Write, draw, dance, sing...express your answers in whatever way feels best to you.

   - Where did you want to stay?
   - Where did you want to leave?
   - What benefits did you experience in the center of the room?
   - How could "living" in the center of the room change your life?
   - How could "living" in the center of the room make for a better world?

The ability to live from different perspectives expands understanding and makes a better world. An integral approach, using all the dimensions of inner knowing, not only brings comfort with and appreciation of differences, but also awareness of similarity and connection. This is the Wisdom of the Whole®.

Afterword

We came together to provide a process that we hope has brought insight, awareness, action, and change. How did it go? What has been your experience?

We would love to hear from you at our book's website: *change.wisdomofthewhole.com* Enter book code: CHANGE7777 to register on our community sharing website.

If you are interested to find out more, we have an award-winning coaching text book, *The Wisdom of the Whole: Coaching for Joy, Health, and Success*, plus a card deck with coaching tools based on the dimensions of life. Use them yourself, with others, or give them as gifts.

Our 60-hour professional coach training is available in person, and via voice-to-voice live video or teleclasses. You can learn more information about the subjects mentioned in our book in the Wisdom of the Whole® coach training program. As a next step, experience our coaching model and sign up for a free 1-hour live video or teleclass at *www.wisdomofthewhole.com/free-class*.

WISDOM OF THE **WHOLE**
COACHING ACADEMY

Thanks to...

Our amazing designer, Becky Lara, who was extremely creative in designing the covers, editing, and doing the layout. She was very patient and masterfully innovative.

Swami Ravi Rudra Bharati (Rudolph Ballentine, MD), who infused this book with his unique insight and wisdom about Jean Gebser's model and how to live from the integral perspective. Transition into this new way of knowing and being takes time and experimentation, and he had much to add about this process.

Our Wisdom of the Whole Team, especially Charlotte Nielsen, who helped with rewriting, fine tuning, and project management, and Ani Stedman, who is our everything master.

Dr. Yi Wu, a preeminent professor of Chinese philosophy at California Institute of Integral Studies, for his understanding of the Platinum Rule on page 26 and his translation about where a journey begins on page 90.

Jay Perry, an outstanding pioneer in coaching, who uses the powerful question on page 88.

Our families and friends, who continue to support our wild ideas and projects.

About the Artwork

This book evolved organically from a series of conversations Linda and Bob had at their favorite hang out in Reno, Nevada: the Gold and Silver Diner. Linda presented Bob with a compilation of powerful questions and statements that are essential to the Wisdom of the Whole coaching model and training. Bob took them home, read them only once, and put them away, allowing them to become part of his subconscious and to work with his intuitive artistic nature. A month later, Bob took out his sketchbook and without prior contemplation, created more than 100 random drawings in a week, each taking shape only at the point that he put pen to paper. Then, Linda and Bob met at the diner and paired the drawings with the statements and questions. The structure of the book came together in the 12 months that followed and was refined over three more years. It was important to them that they not only described the four different ways of knowing (Source, Intuitive, Mythical, and Mental), but that they actually used them to create these pages. Their hope is that they have created an integral book that will invite change to help people transition into the integral way of knowing and being.

About the Author

Linda Bark, PhD, RN, MCC, NC-BC, NBC-HWC has created new professional pathways in coaching and healthcare. In 1970 she was a pioneer in starting a nursing private practice and brought holistic nursing to hospitals in the 1980s. During the next decade, she led medical tours to China, lived in China to discover how to help Westerners create a context for Eastern healing, and consulted for organizations nationwide to start integral/holistic healing centers. Using her coaching model principles, she still works with organizations to build healthy cultures. She continues to teach her Wisdom of the Whole® coaching model internationally at such institutions as Mayo Clinic, Cleveland Clinic, and KPMG in India. She also works in her private practice as a life/health/business/executive/mentor coach. She has an award-winning coaching textbook and has been instrumental in creating national board certifications for both the Nurse Coach and the Health and Wellness Coach. Her formal education includes two nursing degrees, a master's degree in Life Transition Counseling, a certificate in Integral Health Studies, a PhD in Philosophy, and post-graduate studies in Indian Spirituality.

She currently lives in the San Francisco Bay area and frequently travels to rural Nevada to visit her family, where she is involved with her grandchildren's many 4-H projects with goats, rabbits, horses, cats, and dogs. She finds these trips a nice balance to her city life and work.

About the Artist

Throughout his life, Robert Boisson has been a passionate observer, researcher, and creator, particularly within the fields of photography, illustration, and fine art. Added to these pursuits, are a love of nature, a study of psychology, concerns for the human condition, and an acute appreciation for humor in its many strange manifestations, reflected in the unique drawings found in this book.

Bob has exhibited art and photography in numerous gallery and museum shows in California, Nevada, and Arizona. He was invited to curate exhibits for the University of Nevada and what would become the Nevada Museum of Art. He continues to exhibit with photos recently included in a New York City gallery of world-wide photographers and drawings included in a Nevada show entitled, "Identity," in the fall of 2017.

His professional career in advertising, marketing, and media has included positions of creative director and vice president with ad agencies, director of promotion for the nation's newspaper, *USA Today,* and marketing development director for various newspapers within the Gannett company.

He has collaborated with Dr. Linda Bark variously as an artist, writer, and marketing consultant since the 1970s, sharing a desire to help others discover their inner strengths and maximize their abilities to achieve their own unique goals.

Made in the USA
Lexington, KY
30 January 2018